The Way
It All Began!

The Way It All Began!

Pictures by Anthony Lupatelli

Text by Oscar Weigle

Original English language edition published under the title of
ANIMAL ANTICS
by The Hamlyn Publishing Group Limited
© Copyright Piero Dami Editore & Presse Bureau Junior
© Copyright 1974 The Hamlyn Publishing Group Limited
First published in the United States by Grosset & Dunlap, Inc. 1975
Text, U.S. edition Copyright © 1975 by Grosset & Dunlap, Inc.
All Rights Reserved.
Library of Congress Catalog Card Number: 74-17718
ISBN: 0-448-11913-7 (Trade Edition)
ISBN: 0-448-13247-8 (Library Edition)
Printed in the United States of America

GROSSET & DUNLAP • **PUBLISHERS** • **NEW YORK**

The Wheel

Once upon a time, there was no such thing as a wheel. That's hard to believe, but it's true. If you wanted to move something heavy, you had to carry it or pull it. Ugh! Imagine the muscles you'd have to have to drag a big lummox like this!

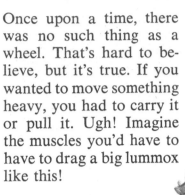

One day someone had a bright idea. A heavy load piled high on a kind of sled was rolled over a line of tree trunks. The sled slid along easily. As soon as a log became free at the back, it was quickly placed in front so that everything could still move forward.

The only trouble with that idea was that the logs wore out very quickly. There had to be a better way!

There was. One day someone sawed off the ends of two trunks, made holes in the center of each circle, and joined them together with a long pole. Some pegs hammered in at the ends of the pole kept the round trunks from falling off. Later on, people called this a wheel and axle. Another long pole tied to the middle of the first one was convenient, because one could hold on to it and even steer the wheel and axle in any direction.

And so the ride was born. For those who could ride, it was much more fun than walking.

The wheel was an instant success. Before long, there were unicycles . . . and wagons . . . and, of course, expert wheel-makers.

Iron

This is a bear story, but it might once have happened the same way with people!

Once there was a home-loving bear who liked nothing better than to fix things up around the house. But he needed tools. Off he went to a toolmaker and bought a heavy hammer.

Because he wanted to protect his head as he worked—things were often falling on him—the bear put a clay pot on his head.

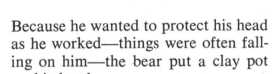

But there were also mean animals around—animals who were bigger, stronger and fiercer than the bear. One such creature swung a club hard. The bear's helmet was broken to bits.

When the bear's head was better again, he lit a fire one day on some hard reddish rock. But when the fire went out, something that looked like stone lay in the embers. Strangely enough, it was soft when it was hot, but hard when it got cold.

Curious, the bear heated the reddish earth in a big oven. As it got hot, it began to flow like liquid, and as it cooled, it hardened. This was exciting! As he experimented, the bear found that as the material cooled, he could twist and hammer it into shape.

This discovery came to be called iron. A blacksmith made a new helmet for the bear out of this new material. Now, instead of having his helmet broken, the bear found that the helmet broke other things!

Back home in his cave, the bear settled down for a long winter's nap. And Mrs. Bear found that the helmet was just fine, too, for making nuts-and-berry soup.

Paper

Once upon a time, when there were no books or newspapers, people would carve pictures on stones. That would help them remember things—or give information to others. But one "book" might weigh as much as a library!

Some people decided not to bother at all. But they were likely to get terrible headaches trying to remember everything!

As time went on, letters and words were invented. They could be written on clay tablets baked in the sun. But—oops!—these tablets were easily dropped and broken.

Someone thought of writing on wax laid on smooth pieces of wood, but when the sun shone bright the wax would melt and the writing would drip away.

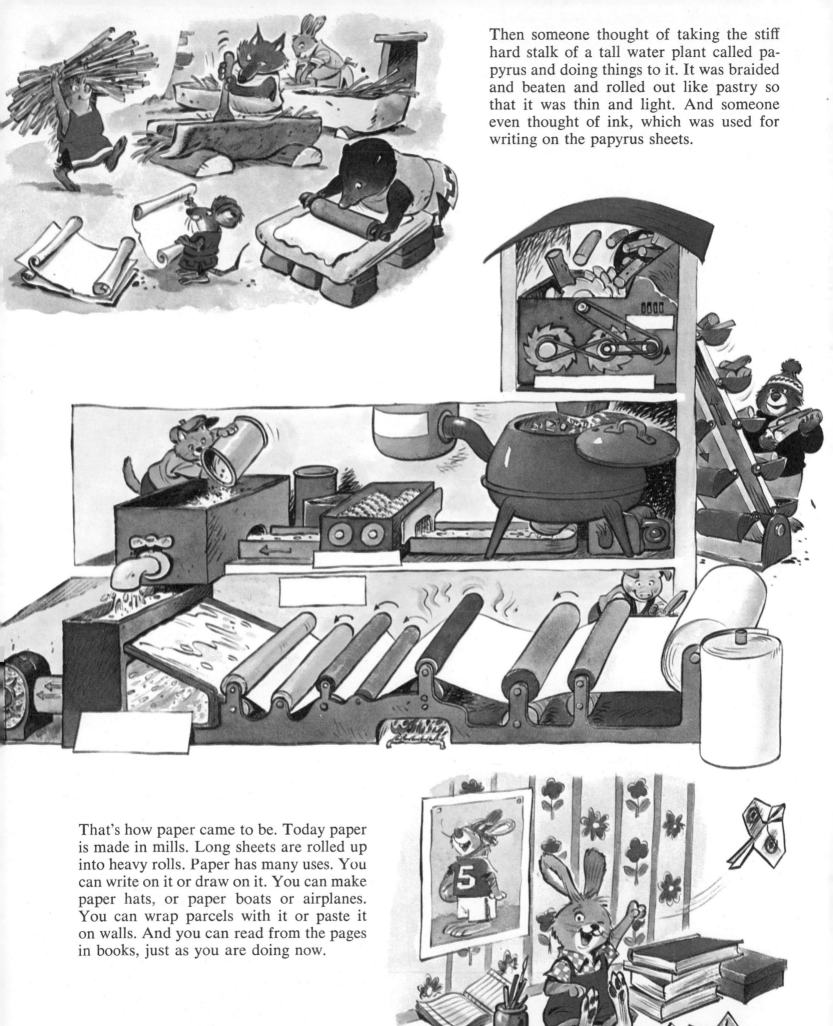

Then someone thought of taking the stiff hard stalk of a tall water plant called papyrus and doing things to it. It was braided and beaten and rolled out like pastry so that it was thin and light. And someone even thought of ink, which was used for writing on the papyrus sheets.

That's how paper came to be. Today paper is made in mills. Long sheets are rolled up into heavy rolls. Paper has many uses. You can write on it or draw on it. You can make paper hats, or paper boats or airplanes. You can wrap parcels with it or paste it on walls. And you can read from the pages in books, just as you are doing now.

Glass

Once there was a potter who decided to try a new way to decorate his pots. He melted sand and silicon, but he was disappointed because the result was a substance without color that you could see through. The potter didn't think it was very useful, but his friend began to make pots and vases out of this material, which was glass. They learned how to make it brightly colored, as well.

Houses didn't have windows at that time, because no one could make glass in sheets. People had to put up wooden shutters to keep out the cold. Of course, that also kept out the light.

How wonderful it was when panes of glass were finally invented! People could look through them and say, "I see you!" and "I see you, too!"

Windows were soon made—either in one large clear piece or with small colored pieces which formed a picture. Sometimes the small pieces were kept in place by strips of lead. Today we have glass that can be either small and delicate or as large as you might imagine.

Matches

One of the first ways of starting a fire was to turn a stick quickly on a piece of wood until a spark was produced, lighting pieces of dry moss laid close to it. The moss, in turn, would light dry sticks. Then more sticks would be added, till the fire blazed.

In some places, later on, people could get a light whenever they needed it from a fire that burned in a public place. But it was hard to get the fire home, because many times the flame would go out in a short time.

Still later, some people used a flint and steel to make sparks, but it wasn't very different from rubbing sticks together. Then there was another way. Small wooden sticks soaked in sulphur were first dipped into a little bottle, and then struck on a stone. It was a way to light a pipe.

One inventor used all kinds of things for his experiments.

His assistant was carrying many of these things one day, including some glue, when he tripped on a broken floorboard and sent everything flying. What a mess!

The inventor's assistant pulled up the loose floorboard and tried to scrape up the mess. He rubbed and pushed. Suddenly there was a flash and a roar, and everything burst into flames. He had made an enormous match! When the inventor made a tiny version of the same thing, matches became popular everywhere.

The Rocket

Rockets are not as new as you might think. Ever so long ago, "rocket arrows" loaded with gunpowder kept an enemy from getting too close in China.

Much later, rockets were used to send letters across valleys and mountains.

Rockets were even used to move an automobile forward at racing speed.

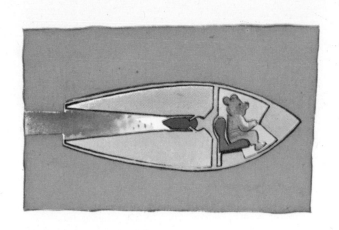

Rockets of the Space Age have been sent high into the air to take pictures and measurements. They have even gone out of earth's atmosphere, to the moon and beyond. Would you like to tour the galaxies in a rocket?

Printing

Writing books by hand took a very long time. And if someone wanted to copy a book, it took even more time. People would spend months, even years, at it. Only the very rich could afford to own books. Then someone thought of printing. Words were written into wet clay with a kind of punch. When the clay dried, liquid lead and tin was poured over it—and when that cooled, a metal plate was formed. When ink was smeared over it, the plate could be pressed down on paper again and again to repeat the original words. Many plates made many pages, and many pages, bound together, made books.

The first books of this kind were disappointing because there were no pictures or colors. It also took many old lead mugs and plates to be melted down to make even one book.

One day an accident happened. The box holding all the punches with the letters was spilled.

The printer's coat (which was where the punches fell) had letters all over it. Why not, thought the printer, make letters on metal stands all the same size, put them together to make words, and print pages straight from them? Then, when all the printing was finished, the pages of type could be taken apart and each letter used again for other pages. And that's just what he did!

The Clock

Probably the first clock in the world was one that told the time of day by a shadow that fell from the light of the sun. The shadow might have been that of a stick. The clock was known as a sundial. That worked well enough on sunny days, but who could know what time it was when it was raining?

Another way of telling time was by means of an hourglass. Sand, or mercury, or liquid, took a measured length of time—usually an hour—to fall through a narrow opening connecting two glass containers.

Later on, clocks that had dials with numbers for each hour and that could be seen far away were built. But they didn't always keep time too well. If they ran too fast, people went home from work too early. If they ran too slow, people went home from work too late.

One night the clock hands were moving so slowly that a clock repairman was called to see what he could do. He climbed up a ladder to the clock tower.

Hours passed, but the repairman didn't come down again. When someone looked in on him, he explained, "I've got time on my hands!"

The Compass

Whee! Buried treasure! How was it found? Well, there was an old pirates' map that showed the right island and the right place.

To reach the island, a compass was quite helpful. A compass can tell a sailor the direction his ship is sailing.

Before there were compasses, sailors depended upon Polaris, the North Star, to tell them which way was north. But it did them no good on cloudy nights—or in the daytime.

One man found out that if a piece of magnetic iron was placed in water on a piece of wood, it always pointed north. That was the basic compass.

Of course, you must be careful not to have any other kind of metal close to your compass. It's possible for the needle to be pointing to, say, a frying pan instead of north in such a case. That would be no help at all if you were lost.

The Airship

What a beautiful day for flying! Why not take a ride in a hot-air balloon? This is the type of balloon used in France a long time ago.

1783 MONTGOLFIER

GIFFARD 1852

Another Frenchman designed a long cigar-shaped airship. It wasn't easy to pilot, though. It was especially hard to land.

An umbrella for a parachute? It doesn't really work too well. But if nobody cares how unsafe it might be, balloon riding could seem like lots of fun!

EXPOSITION DE PARIS 1878

The Parachute

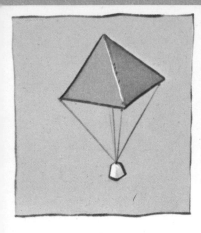 

Leonardo da Vinci, who was a great painter, sculptor, engineer, and scientist, was the first man to see the value of a parachute as a useful invention. He drew sketches of flying machines, as well as parachutes.

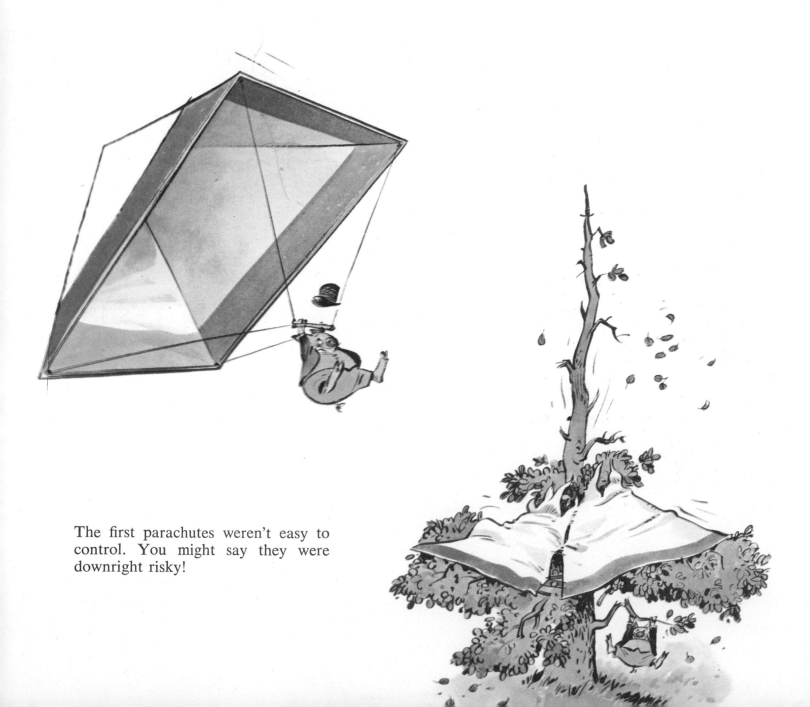

The first parachutes weren't easy to control. You might say they were downright risky!

But as time passed, better parachutes were made. Oh, it was still an adventure, and one had to be brave to jump, but at last the jumps by parachute became much safer.

The Bicycle

What did the first bicycle look like? Well, it was little more than two wheels joined together by a length of wood that served as a seat. How did the bicycle move? Well, to make it go, you sat down gently, put your feet on the ground, and tiptoed along as fast as you could. It was like sitting down and walking at the same time.

Stopping the bicycle could sometimes be a problem. If your feet got sore from dragging them, you could try tossing out a heavy stone that had been tied to the machine and hope that it would do the trick at the right moment.

A ship's anchor thrown from the back of the bicycle to the ground might also be a way of stopping it. But that's risky, too. The problem of moving—and stopping—was solved in time by the bicycle chain and pedals.

The Railroad

The wheel was a wonderful invention. But getting it to turn always required effort on the part of someone. How much better it would be if it could be made to turn mechanically! New power was needed, perhaps the kind that could lift the lid on a kettle of boiling water.

The idea was worth trying. A "steam engine" invented by a Frenchman managed to power a vehicle on the road, but unfortunately it smashed to pieces after only a few hours. Other steam cars were built, but a ride along rough and uneven roads was anything but comfortable. Then someone thought of building rails that reached from place to place, and upon which wheels could run along smoothly.

When that was done, *there* was the first railroad! What fun it is to ride a train! The first passengers thought so, too—even though they got covered with soot as they traveled!

Electricity

Long ago, in Greece, a strange discovery was made. It was found that when a piece of amber was rubbed, it attracted leaves, bits of straw, and other small objects. The word for amber was *elektron,* so it seemed only natural to call the mysterious ways of amber *electric*.

One way to produce a current was to have discs of copper and zinc piled on top of one another and separated by pieces of felt soaked in weak acid. That could give someone a shock, too!

Many years later it was demonstrated that a powerful force known as a "current" could be produced. It had to be carefully handled, though, because if you were careless for even a moment, you could get a shock!

Today, electricity is produced in large amounts. One way is to have moving water turn turbines, which in turn generate electricity for our needs.

Electricity lights our homes, runs all sorts of appliances, and keeps machines going in factories. We usually miss it as soon as it is not available.

Frayed electric cords are dangerous. One must never handle them—or any exposed wires—when they are "plugged in."

The Steamship

When there were no engines in ships and boats, sailing along in bad weather was no fun at all. And in calm weather, even sailing ships could use some extra help in moving along.

People thought of many ways to move a boat through water. Silly ways, too. But Robert Fulton thought of a practical way of putting a steam engine and paddle wheel onto a ship. Then things really moved! Let's hear it for Robert Fulton!

HAPPY★STAR

The Electric Light Bulb

For thousands of years the only light people had at night came from the moon, or torches, or campfires, or oil lamps. Oil lamps and candles are still used today, but in many places they are used mainly for a decorative effect. Later on, gas was used to light the streets and people's houses. It was brighter than anything used before, but it was also somewhat dangerous.

Thomas A. Edison, a famous inventor, wondered if electricity could be used for lighting. A very fine wire made of carbon was put in a glass bulb that had no air in it. An electric current passing through the wire made it glow brightly from produced heat. The light at first was weak and wavering, but it was soon improved.

Today there are many different types of light bulbs. They are at home and on the streets. Powerful beacons guide ships and airplanes. Lights are on cars, trucks and trains. Shows depend on lights. And so does anyone lost in the woods at night!

The Submarine

For a long time men dreamed of building some kind of craft that would travel under water. The leaders of armies and navies naturally thought of such a craft as something that could sink enemy ships. Many designs were drawn up, but not many of them proved to be practical.

In time, however, the submarine was developed, and today it is a marvelous way of traveling under water—and even under arctic ice! It has a periscope, which allows people inside to see what is happening on the surface of the water. It also has a gyroscope, which shows which way it is going, and all kinds of equipment to keep it safe and comfortable.

Photography

In olden days, a picture of a person, place or thing was obtained by hiring a talented artist to paint it. Sometimes the painter used a kind of wooden model with clothes draped over it for the body, and painted only the face from his real sitter. Still, it took many, many hours to complete.

In a way, photography really began when it was discovered that light passing through a small hole in a closed box resulted in a projected upside-down image.

Very gradually, through many stages, it was found that such images could be kept for a time on metal plates, brought forth with chemicals, and transferred to paper.

That was how the photograph was born. At first, people had to stand still for a long time. But one no longer had to be rich to get a picture of himself. Today, of course, pictures can be taken faster than saying "Cheese."

The Automobile

What is that contraption we see pictured in the museum? It's a picture of the first vehicle that moved along a road by steam. Somehow, it didn't last very long, perhaps because people didn't trust it, or didn't like it. But they did like a larger version of the steam car that held eighteen people. (It was more like a bus!) Perhaps that was because it was so grand and elaborate. Or perhaps it was fun because it was a sort of motorized hayride.

The engine turned out to be the most convenient way to power a machine on the road. The first of these cars looked like the old carriages that had been pulled by horses, so they were called "horseless carriages."

Antique cars are interesting to see. Some collections have cars of different countries. It's fun to visit them, if you can. A fast modern car is also fun!

The Telegraph

Long ago, people used drumbeats, or fire, or smoke signals, or mirrors that flashed in the sunlight, to send messages to places some distance away. Then signaling devices were built, placed on top of tall towers so that they could be seen. By moving the "arms" to various positions, each position standing for a different letter of the alphabet, words could be spelled out. And, usually, a message had many words.

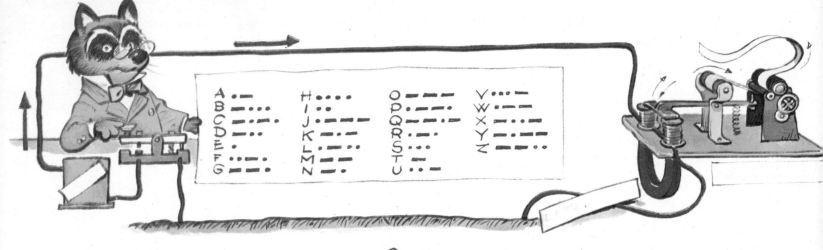

A man named Samuel Morse made up an alphabet that could be heard by means of "short" or "long" clicks. A short click was called a dot; a long click was called a dash. Different combinations of dots and dashes stood for each letter of the regular alphabet, and so words could be spelled out quickly and easily by means of electrical "taps" that traveled along wires. The wires were strung on wooden poles that were placed in the ground.

This was called the telegraph. The alphabet of dot-dash letters came to be called the Morse code. People found that they didn't always have to hear this alphabet to understand a message. If dots and dashes are seen as, say, short or long bursts of light, they can also spell out words.

As America moved westward, so did the telegraph poles. The Old West and the East had an instant way of "keeping in touch."

The Record Player

Before there were record players, if you wanted to hear music, you would either have to play an instrument yourself or else listen to others playing.

Thomas Edison invented a machine called the phonograph. He set up his machine and invited musicians to play songs right next to it.

Were they surprised when their own music was played back to them? They probably were! In time, recordings were made on a flat disc made of wax, and people could listen to music or singing in their own homes. The sound was made louder by being sent through a large horn.

The Telephone

The American Indians had a way of knowing if someone was approaching —they simply put their ears to the ground and listened for the sound of hoofbeats a long way away.

Sound can travel in all sorts of ways. It can even go up the chimney, like smoke. It can be heard along the eaves of houses. (That's how "eavesdrop" came to mean what it does.)

When we use the telephone, our voice sends out sound vibrations that are turned into an electrical current by means of an electromagnet. After the current is sent along wires, it is transformed back to the original vibrations, or sound. In this way, people at either end of the wire can talk to one another, no matter how far apart.

The Airplane

People have always dreamed of being able to fly like a bird.

Leonardo da Vinci, a talented painter and architect, once drew up plans and built models of a flying machine.

Later on, other inventors developed their own ideas for flying ships.

It wasn't until December 17, 1903, that an airplane actually got off the ground and landed by itself. It took place at Kitty Hawk, North Carolina. The plane was built by two brothers named Wright.

Movies

The shadow play was an old form of entertainment in which shadows of puppet figures danced and moved about on a screen. The shadows were produced from a light that was located behind cardboard-cutout figures and projected toward the back of the screen.

When pictures could be made by cameras, it was discovered that if you ran a whole series of pictures together very fast, an illusion of movement in the picture was produced. Movies today produce the same illusion by means of reels of film and projectors.

"Moving pictures" in the beginning were short. They were also without sound, and so today they are sometimes called "silent pictures." But usually a piano player would play music while the pictures were being shown. By playing softly or loudly, slowly or fast, he could set the mood in sound, according to what was being shown at the time. When sound was added directly to film, movies became known as "talking pictures."

Radio

Radio is a wonderful way of sending sounds and messages across distances. It is used all over the world. People in the most out-of-the-way places, like lighthouses, or on small islands—or anywhere else on earth—can keep in touch with everybody else. Radio is also useful in sending emergency messages to policemen, firemen, doctors, and hospitals.

If a ship at sea should be in danger of sinking, you may be sure that the radio operator would send an "S.O.S." That's a call for help from a ship in distress. These letters were chosen because they are easy to send in a wireless code: three dots, three dashes, three dots.

If you can send a message by radio, you can be rescued.

Some people talk to each other by means of "walkie-talkies."

Television

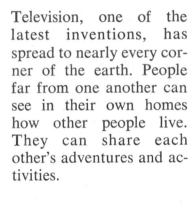

Television, one of the latest inventions, has spread to nearly every corner of the earth. People far from one another can see in their own homes how other people live. They can share each other's adventures and activities.

Television cameras can go almost anywhere.

They can go deep into space and send pictures back to earth.

When necessary, television can be a "watchdog," watching over people in stores, factories and offices.

X-Rays

X-rays are powerful invisible rays that can "see" right through the flesh of people's bodies to the bones of the skeleton.

If somebody should swallow something, such as a key, X-rays can show exactly where it is. But toys will always be better playthings than X-rays.

Jet Airplanes

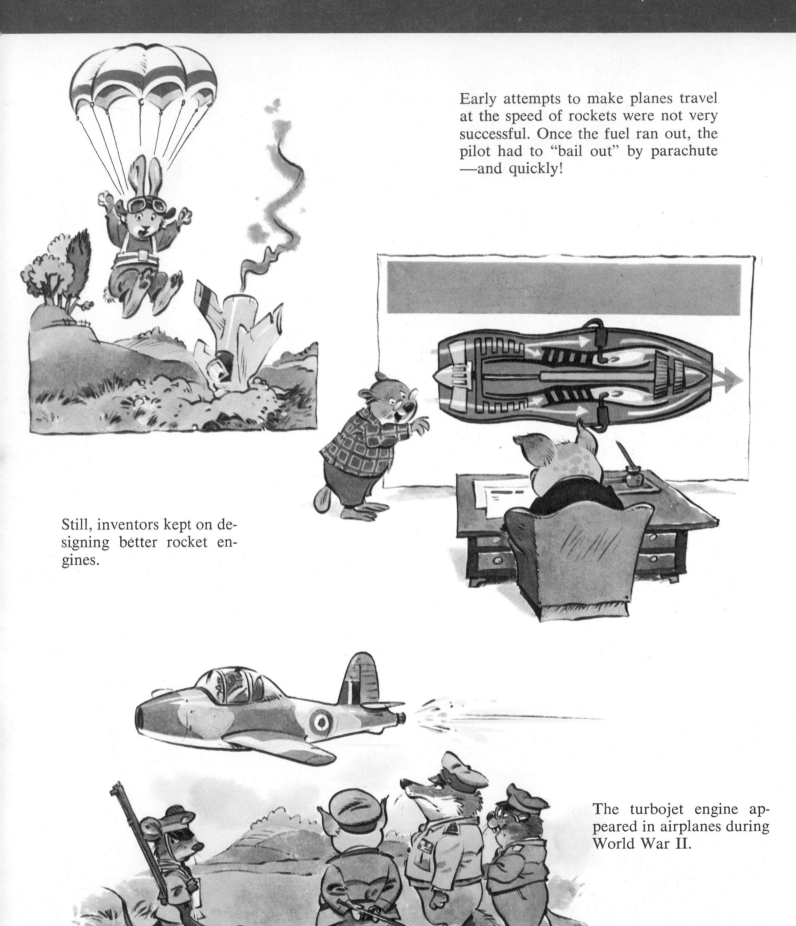

Early attempts to make planes travel at the speed of rockets were not very successful. Once the fuel ran out, the pilot had to "bail out" by parachute —and quickly!

Still, inventors kept on designing better rocket engines.

The turbojet engine appeared in airplanes during World War II.

Eventually, jet travel became commonplace. Hundreds of people could fly across an ocean in one plane!

Some planes can fly faster than sound, and when this happens there is a tremendous shock wave of sound that's heard on the ground as a loud BANG!

BANG!